COPYRIGHT 2019 BY FIDDLEFOX
CREATED BY CHRISTOPHER VUK AND PHIL BERMAN
COLLECTED AND TRANSLATED BY PHIL BERMAN AND NAYRA LOPES
ILLUSTRATIONS BY GABRIELA ISSA-CHACÓN
MUSIC PRODUCTION BY MARC DIAZ

NO PART OF THIS BOOK MAY BE USED OR REPRODUCED IN ANY MANNER
WHATSOEVER UNLESS WRITTEN PERMISSION IS RECEIVED
ALL RIGHTS RESERVED

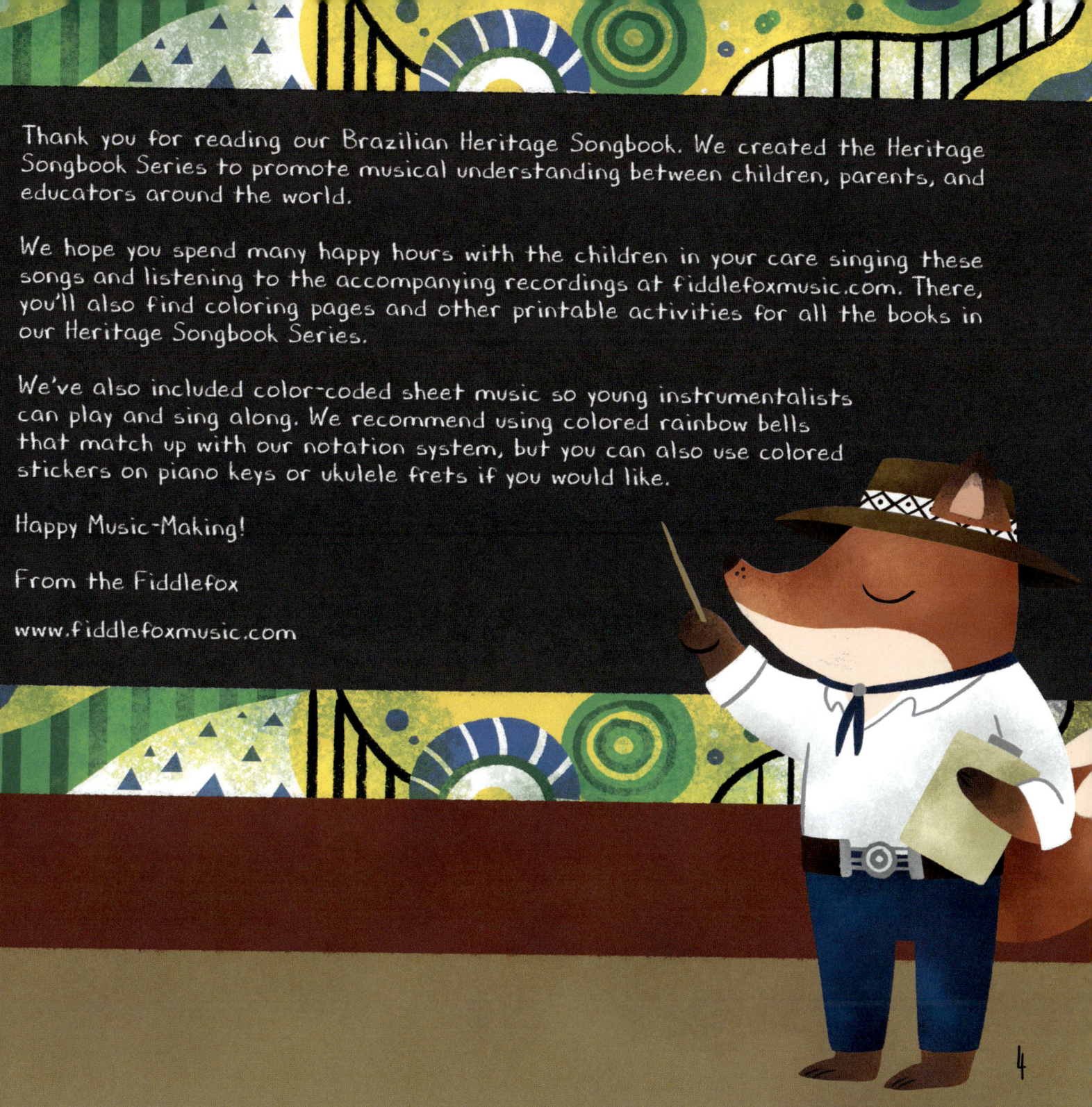

Thank you for reading our Brazilian Heritage Songbook. We created the Heritage Songbook Series to promote musical understanding between children, parents, and educators around the world.

We hope you spend many happy hours with the children in your care singing these songs and listening to the accompanying recordings at fiddlefoxmusic.com. There, you'll also find coloring pages and other printable activities for all the books in our Heritage Songbook Series.

We've also included color-coded sheet music so young instrumentalists can play and sing along. We recommend using colored rainbow bells that match up with our notation system, but you can also use colored stickers on piano keys or ukulele frets if you would like.

Happy Music-Making!

From the Fiddlefox

www.fiddlefoxmusic.com

TABLE OF CONTENTS

	PAGE	CD TRACK
HOW TO USE THIS BOOK	4	
WELCOME TO BRAZIL	7	
SAPO JURURU	9	1
O PIÃO	17	2
CARANGUEJO	25	3
A CANOA VIROU	33	4
SAPO JURURU (KARAOKE)		5
O PIÃO (KARAOKE)		6
CARANGUEJO (KARAOKE)		7
A CANOA VIROU (KARAOKE)		8

Brazilian Heritage Songbook

Brazilians speak Portuguese and love to play soccer (futebol) in their spare time. Brazil is a very diverse country, with a mix of native groups and immigrants from Africa, Europe, and Asia. These different cultures mixed together and created unique types of music like Samba, and a combination of martial arts and dance (Capoeira.)

Brazil is home to more species of animals than any other country on the planet, thanks largely to the Amazon Rainforest. The 40,000 species of Amazonian plants produce 20% of the oxygen we breathe on Earth. Running through the rainforest is the Amazon river, a network of hundreds of waterways that make the longest river in the world.

Today, growing industry poses a threat to the survival of the rainforest and the thousands of species within it. With our choices, our actions, and our voices, we can work together to protect the Amazon and rainforests around the globe.

SAPO JURURU
LITTLE MISTER FROG

Sapo jururu, na beira do rio
Little Mister Frog, crying by the river

Quando o sapo canta, ô maninha
When you sing out loud, oh my darling

É PORQUE TEM FRIO.
DO YOU SHAKE AND SHIVER?

A MULHER DO SAPO DEVE ESTAR LÁ DENTRO
LITTLE MISSUS FROG SITTING ON YOUR BEDDING

Fazendo rendinha, Ô maninha
Making up your lace, oh my darling,

Para o casamento
Ready for your wedding

NOTES USED

D E F G A B C

SAPO JURURU
LITTLE MISTER FROG

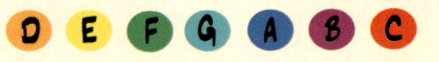

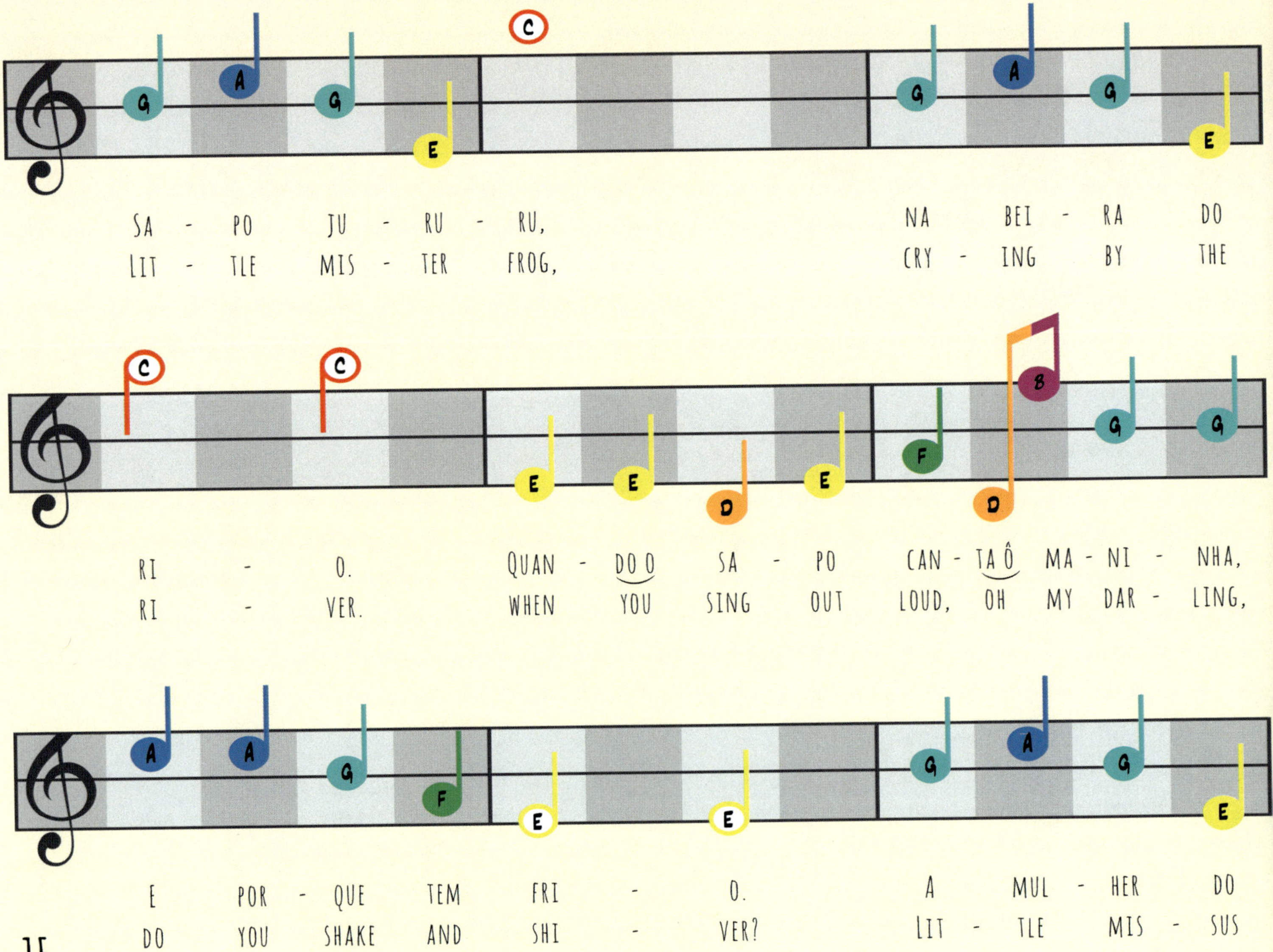

C C G A G E C C
SA - PO DE VE ES - TAR LA DEN - TRO
FROG, ___ SIT - TING ON HER BED - DING
E E D E F D B G G
FA - ZEN - DO RE - DIN - HA, Ô MA - NI - NHA,
MA - KING UP YOUR LACE, OH MY DAR - LING,
B B A B C C
PAR - A O CA - SA - MEN - TO.
REA - DY FOR YOUR WED - DING.

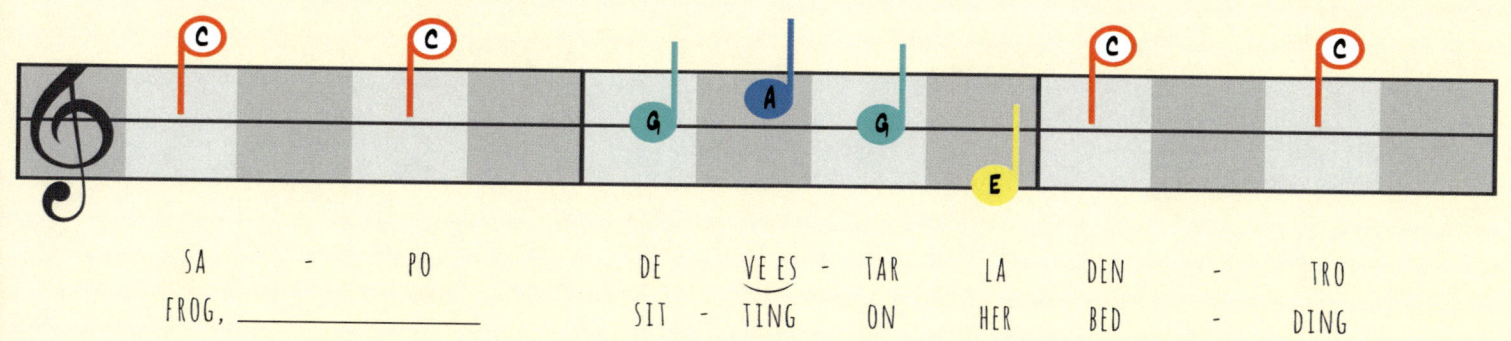

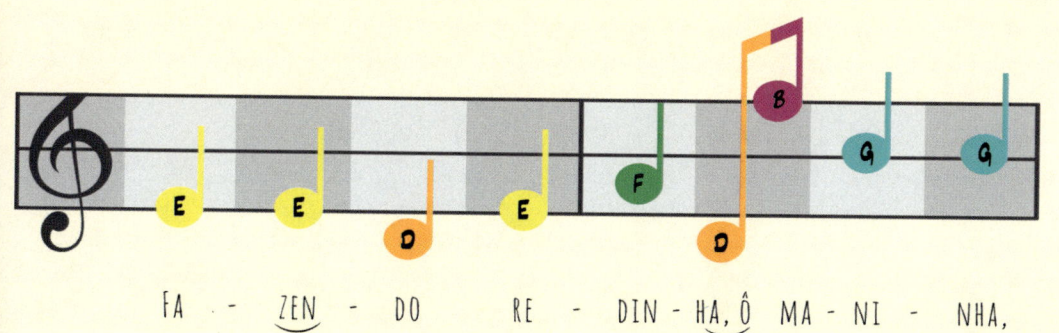

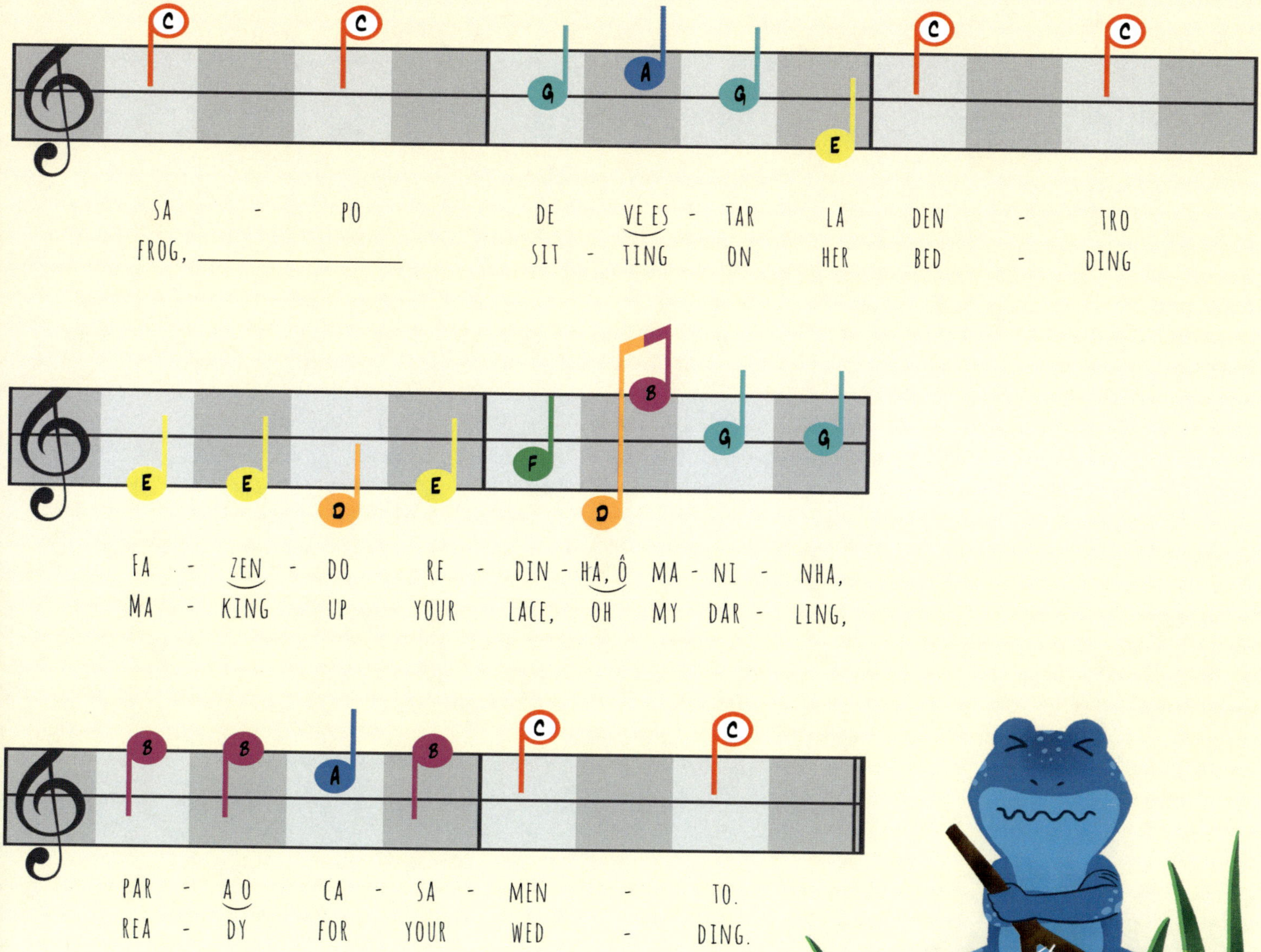

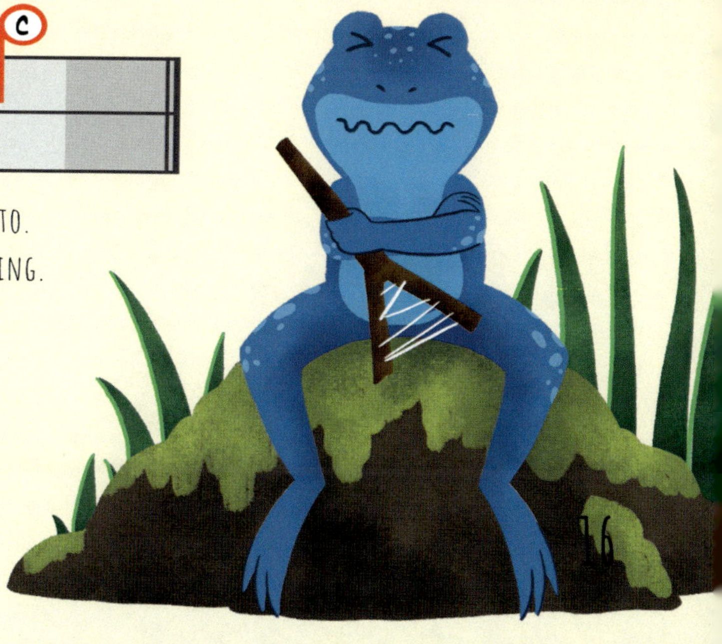

Roda pião, bambeia pião
Spin for me now, a-wobblin' down

Roda pião, bambeia pião
Spin for me now,
a-wobblin' down

O PIÃO
THE TOP

BRAZILIAN TRADITIONAL

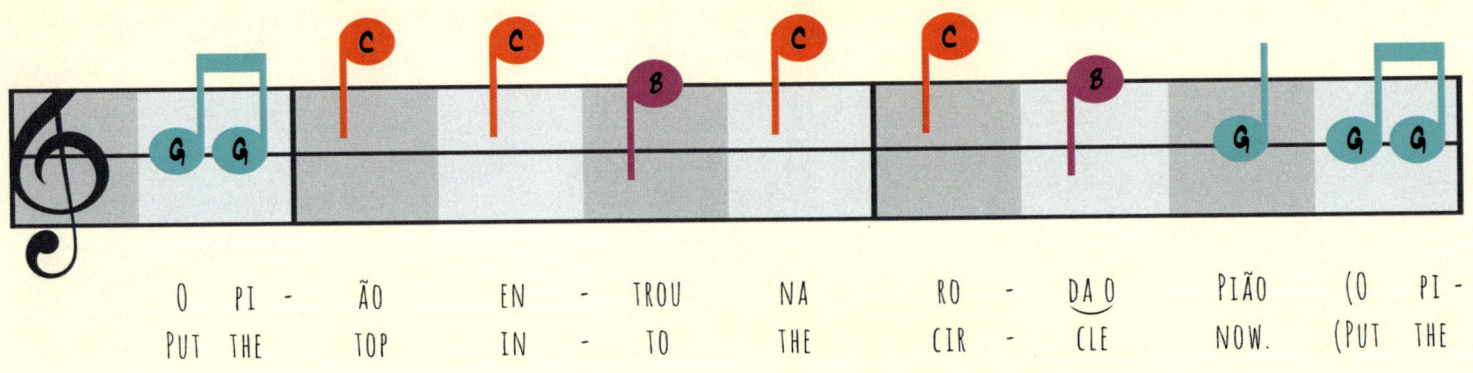
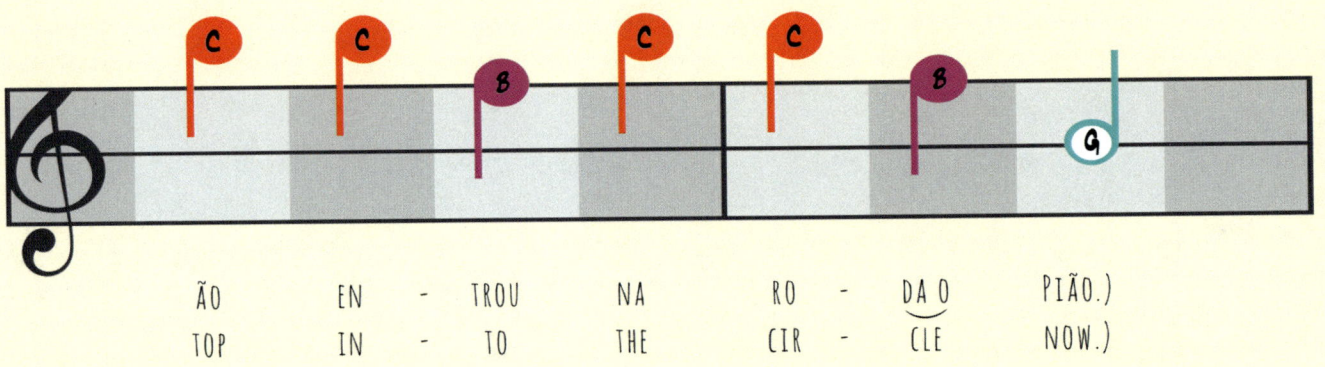

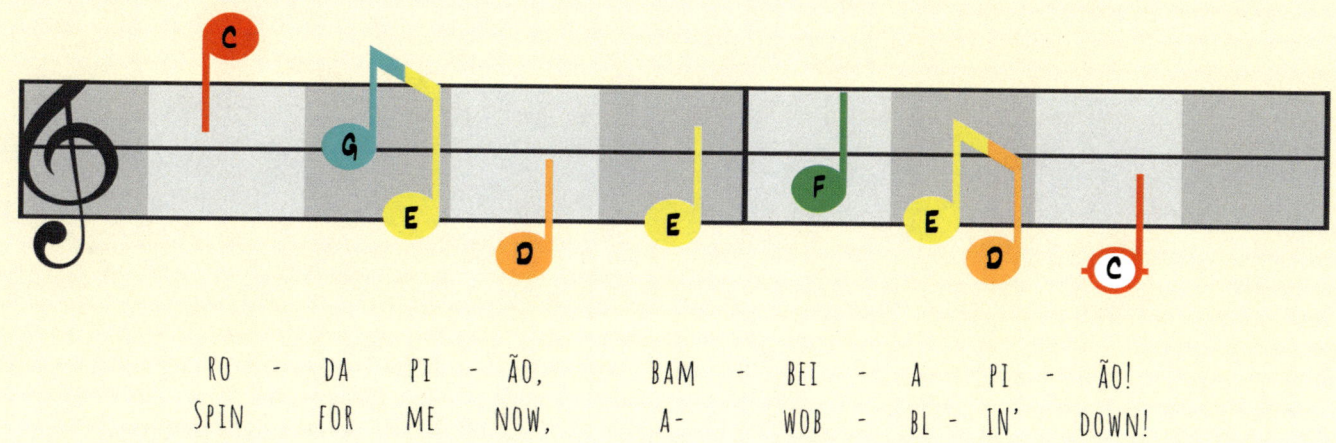

RO - DA PI - ÃO, BAM - BEI - A PI - ÃO!
SPIN FOR ME NOW, A- WOB - BL - IN' DOWN!

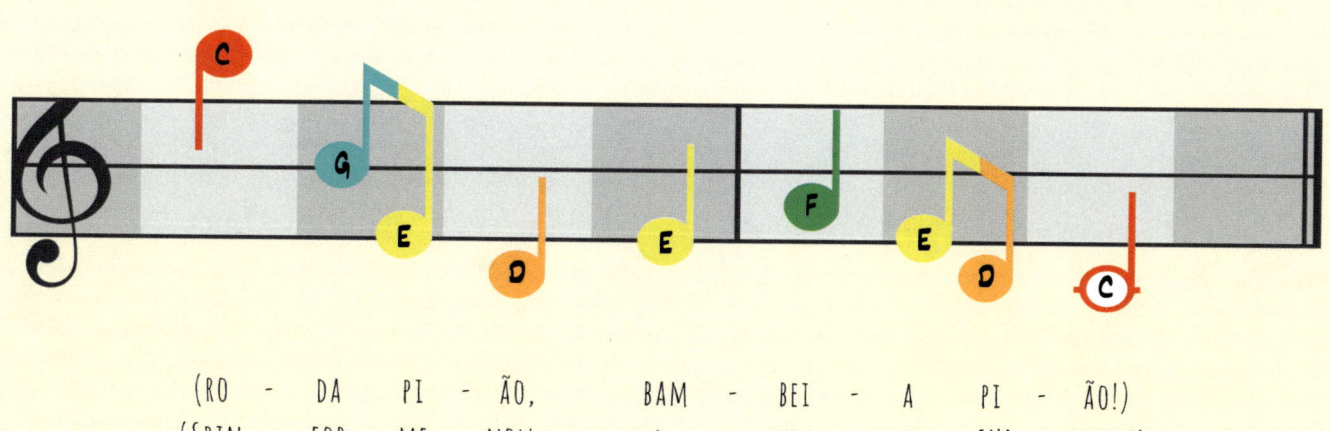

(RO - DA PI - ÃO, BAM - BEI - A PI - ÃO!)
(SPIN FOR ME NOW, A- WOB - BL - IN' DOWN!)

CARANGUEJO
THE CRAB

Caranguejo não é peixe
Oh the crab is not a fishy!

Caranguejo só é peixe na enchente da maré
Oh the crab is only fishy when the tide is really high

Ora palma, palma, palma
He can clap it, clap it, clap it

Ora pé, pé, pé
He can swish, swish, swish

Ora roda, roda, roda,
He can turn, and turn, and turn

Caranguejo peixe é
I say the crab, he is a fish

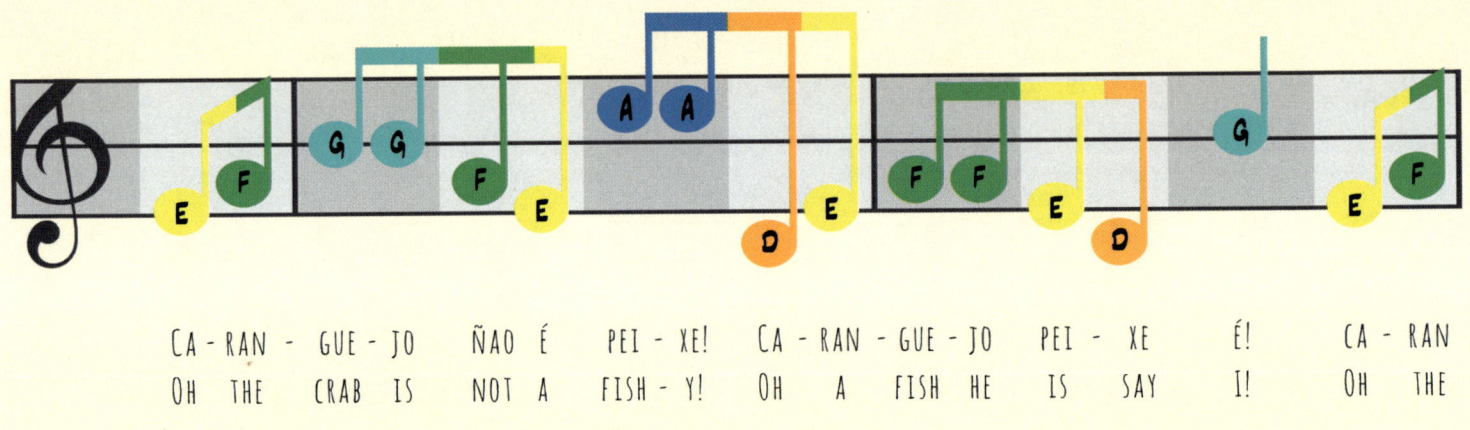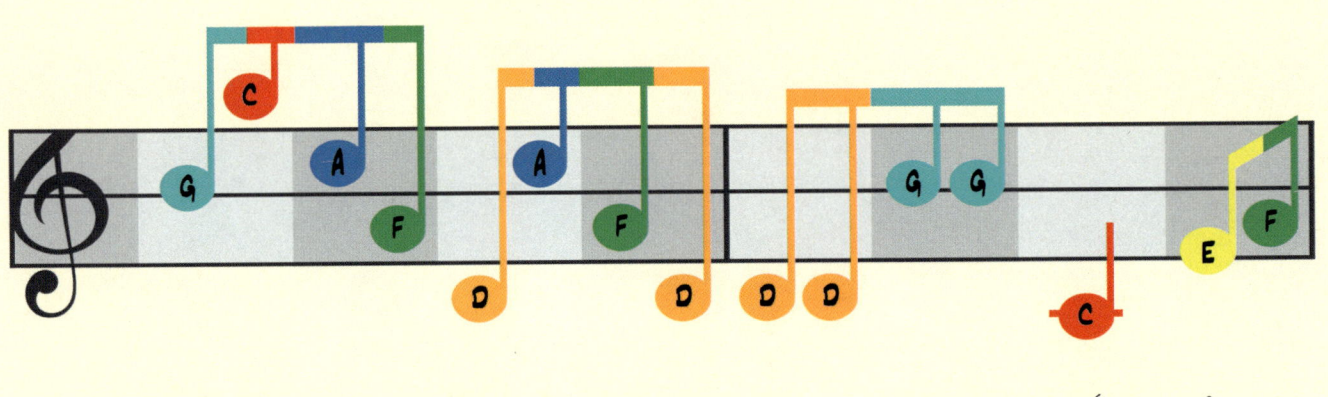

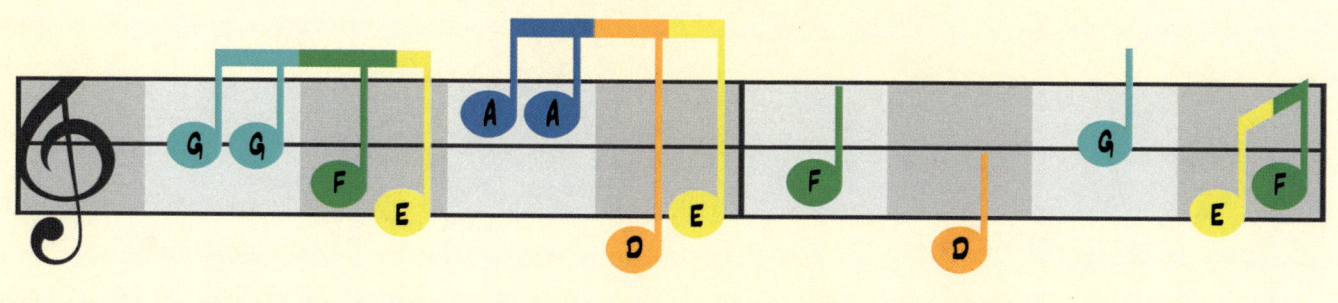

PAL - MA, PAL - MA, PAL - MA. O - RA PÉ, PÉ, PÉ. O - RA
CLAP IT, CLAP IT, CLAP IT! HE CAN SWISH, SWISH, SWISH! HE CAN

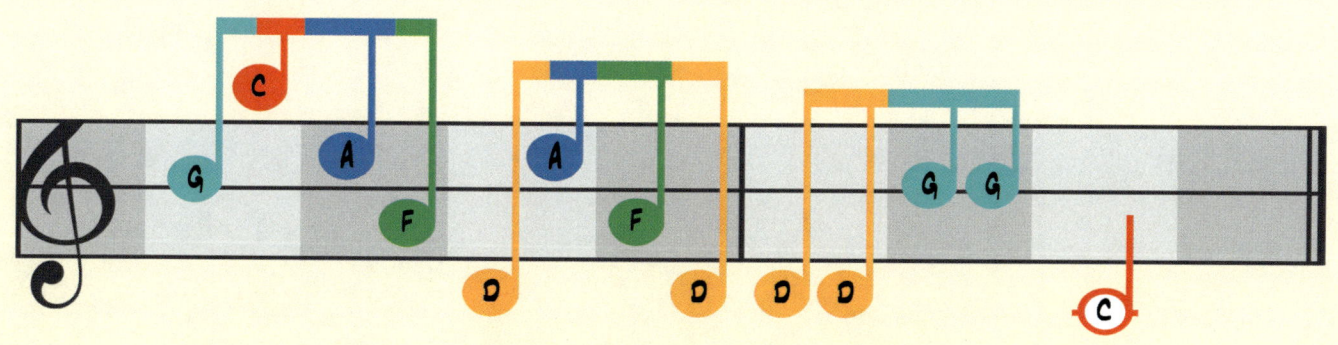

RO - DA, RO - DA, RO - DA, CA - RAN GUE JO, PEI XE É.
TURN, AND TURN, AND TURN, I SAY THE CRAB, HE IS A FISH.

A CANOA VIROU
WE FLIPPED THE CANOE

A canoa virou
When we flipped the canoe

Quem deixou ela virar
We could tell who let us go

Foi por causa do Lorenzo
It's because of Lorenzo

Que não soube remar
That we don't know how to row!

Se eu fouce um peixinho
And if I was a fish

Que soubesse nadar
Swimming deep and swimming free

Eu tirava o Lorenzo do fundo do mar.
I would go to get Lorenzo from under the sea.

BRAZILIAN TRADITIONAL

A CANOA VIROU
WE FLIPPED THE CANOE

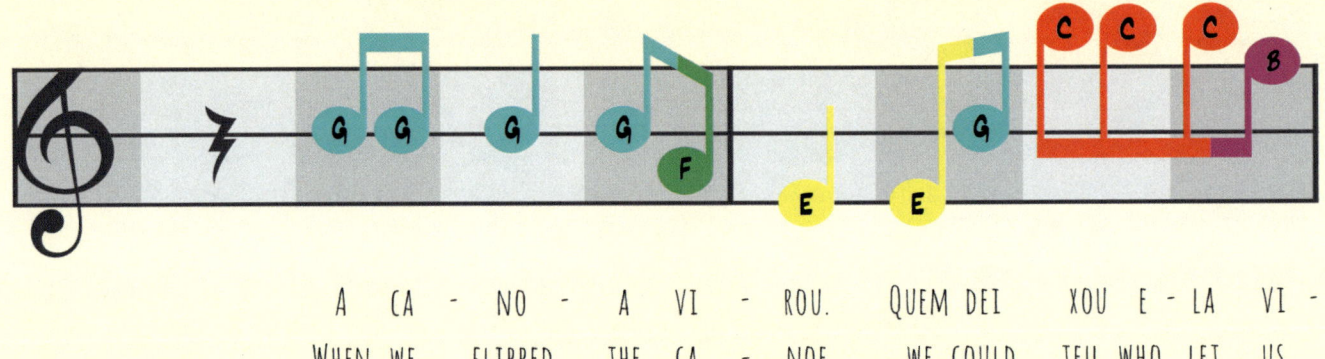

A CA - NO - A VI - ROU. QUEM DEI XOU E - LA VI -
When we flipped the ca - noe we could tell who let us

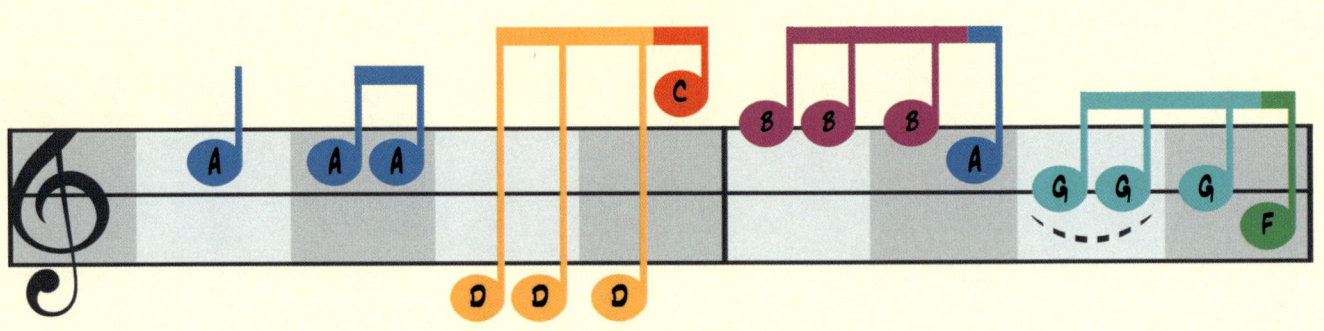

RAR? FOI POR CAU - SA DO LO - REN - ZO QUE NÃO SOU - BE - RE -
GO, IT'S BE - CAUSE___ OF LO - REN - ZO THAT WE DON'T KNOW HOW TO

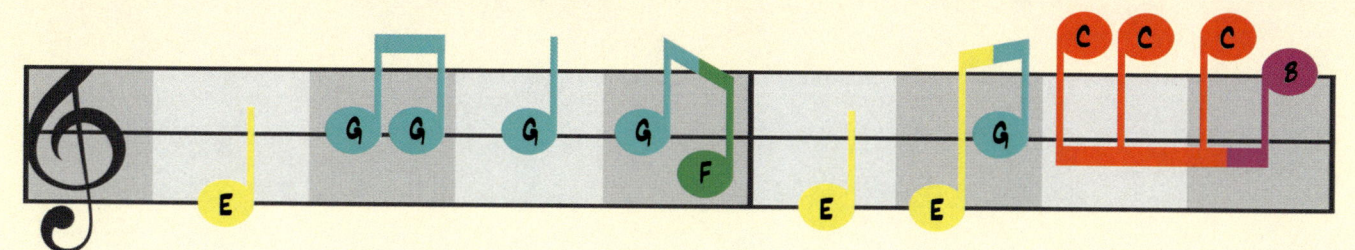

MAR. SE EU FOU-CE UM PEI-XIN-HO QUE SOU-BE-SSE NA-
ROW! AND IF I - WAS A FISH SWIM-MING DEEP AND SWIM-ING

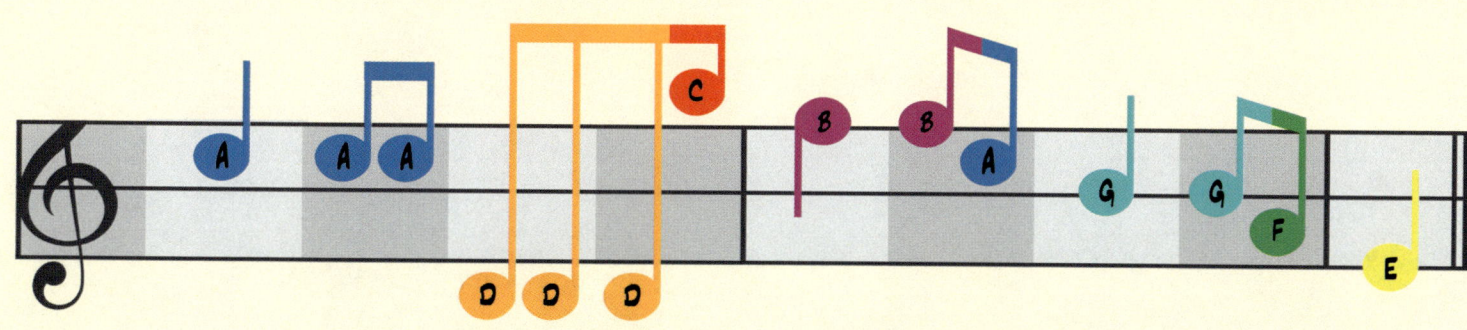

DAR EU TI-RA-VA O LO-REN-ZO DO FUN-DO DO MAR.
FREE, I WOULD GO TO GET LO-REN-ZO FROM UN-DER THE SEA.

BRING A WORLD OF MUSIC HOME WITH FIDDLEFOX WORLD HERITAGE SONGBOOKS!

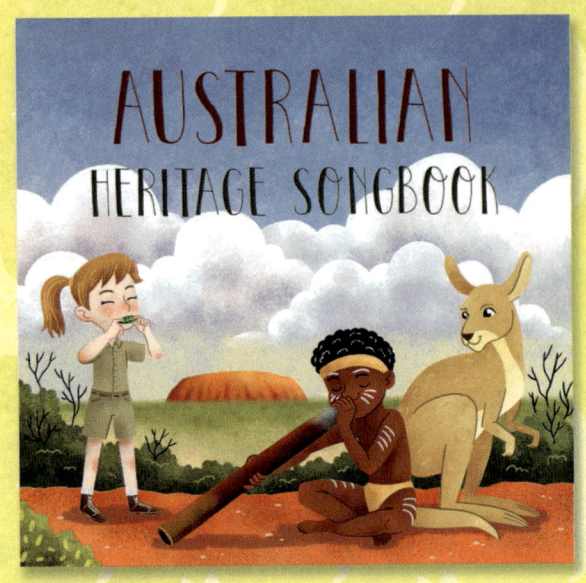

Available on iBooks, Kindle and Spotify!
www.fiddlefoxmusic.com